Copyright © Micah-Daniels Gbenga

Table of Contents

Economic devastation, a term that carries weight and echoes with consequences, refers to the widespread and profound disruption of a nation's financial and economic systems. It encompasses a multifaceted range of challenges that can arise from various triggers, including financial crises, natural disasters, global pandemics, or a combination of these factors. When economic devastation strikes, the repercussions ripple through industries, livelihoods, and communities, leaving a lasting imprint on the socioeconomic fabric of a country. This book delves into the complexities of economic devastation, shedding light on its causes, effects, and the strategies nations and individuals employ to rebuild and emerge stronger from the aftermath. As we explore the dynamics of economic devastation, we uncover the resilience and adaptability of societies in the face of adversity and the lessons that can guide us toward more robust and sustainable economic systems.

Definition of a Devastating Economy

A devastating economy refers to a state of severe and widespread economic distress characterized by significant negative impacts on key economic indicators such as gross domestic product (GDP), unemployment rates, inflation, poverty levels, and overall economic stability. In a devastating economy, various factors, including financial crises, external shocks, natural disasters, geopolitical instability, or systemic failures, converge to create a prolonged period of economic decline, hardship, and disruption. This state often entails a sharp contraction of economic activity, loss of jobs and livelihoods, decreased consumer spending, reduced business investment, and challenges in accessing essential services and resources. The consequences of a devastating economy can have far-reaching implications for individuals, businesses, communities, and the overall socio-political landscape of a nation.

A devastating economy is a dire and challenging state that emerges when a nation faces a significant and prolonged downturn in its economic performance. This situation is marked by a cascade of adverse events that collectively undermine the stability, growth, and well-being of a country's economy. Such circumstances can be triggered by a variety of factors, including financial crises, natural disasters, geopolitical conflicts, global pandemics, or a combination of these and other unforeseen events.

During a devastating economy, several critical economic indicators experience sharp declines or disruptions. These indicators include:

1. Gross Domestic Product (GDP): The total value of all goods and

services produced within a country's borders. In a devastating economy, GDP contracts, leading to reduced economic output and a potential recession.

2. Unemployment Rates: A significant rise in unemployment as businesses struggle to maintain operations, leading to job cuts and decreased hiring. This results in increased joblessness and underemployment, with ripple effects on household incomes and consumer spending.

3. Inflation: While economic devastation can lead to deflation (a decrease in general price levels), certain factors such as supply chain disruptions may cause inflation, making it difficult for individuals to afford essential goods and services.

4. Business Closures and Bankruptcies: Many businesses, particularly small and medium-sized enterprises, face financial strain and may have to shut down operations due to reduced demand and financial difficulties.

5. Consumer Spending: As individuals experience uncertainty about their economic prospects, they tend to reduce discretionary spending, causing a decline in consumption that further dampens economic activity.

6. Government Revenue and Budget Deficits: A shrinking economy results in decreased tax revenue for the government, making it challenging to fund public services and initiatives. This often leads to budget deficits and reduced public investments.

7. Financial Instability: Economic devastation can trigger financial market turmoil, with stock market crashes, banking crises, and disruptions in the credit market.
8. Social and Welfare Programs: Increased unemployment and poverty rates place additional strain on social safety nets and welfare programs as more individuals and families require support.

A devastating economy has wide-ranging societal impacts, including increased poverty and inequality, social unrest, strained healthcare and educational systems, and challenges in maintaining basic infrastructure. However, history shows that nations can recover and rebuild from such conditions through concerted efforts, adaptive policies, and collective resilience. By implementing effective recovery strategies, addressing root causes, and fostering a supportive environment for innovation and entrepreneurship, societies can navigate the challenges of a devastating economy and work towards a more stable and prosperous future.

Economic devastation, with its far-reaching implications and profound societal consequences, underscores the critical importance of proactive and strategic measures to address and mitigate its impact. When a nation's economy is plunged into turmoil, the repercussions extend beyond financial markets and economic indicators, permeating every facet of society. Recognizing and promptly addressing economic devastation is not only a matter of economic stability but also a fundamental imperative for social well-being, political harmony, and sustainable progress. Here's why addressing economic devastation is of paramount importance:

1. Preserving Livelihoods and Well-being: At the core of economic devastation lies the erosion of jobs, livelihoods, and financial security for countless individuals and families. Addressing economic distress means safeguarding people's ability to provide for themselves and their loved ones, preventing the exacerbation of poverty, and preserving the dignity and well-being of citizens.

2. Mitigating Social Unrest: A deteriorating economy often correlates with increased social tension and unrest. High unemployment rates, reduced access to basic services, and declining living standards can create a breeding ground for frustration, disillusionment, and even social conflict. Addressing economic devastation helps

maintain social cohesion and stability, contributing to a more harmonious society.

3. Fostering Political Stability: Economic turmoil can strain political institutions and governance structures. Addressing economic challenges helps prevent political instability and potential power struggles that can arise from citizens' dissatisfaction with their leaders' inability to manage the economy effectively.

4. Safeguarding Human Capital: A robust and thriving economy is intertwined with investments in education, healthcare, and human development. When an economy faces devastation, these crucial sectors are often adversely affected. By addressing economic distress, societies protect their human capital, ensuring access to

quality education, healthcare, and opportunities for personal growth.

5. Restoring Confidence and Investor Trust: A nation's economic health significantly influences global perception and investor confidence. Addressing economic devastation demonstrates a commitment to stability and resilience, which can attract foreign investment, stimulate economic growth, and contribute to long-term prosperity.

6. Economic Resilience: By tackling the root causes of economic devastation, countries can build resilience to future shocks. Learning from past experiences, implementing robust policies, and diversifying economic activities create a more agile and adaptable economic environment.

7. Opportunity for Innovation and Reform: Economic crises can serve as catalysts for innovation, prompting governments, businesses, and individuals to rethink existing structures and systems. Addressing economic devastation offers an opportunity to enact structural reforms that enhance economic efficiency, promote sustainable growth, and drive positive change.

8. Long-Term Prosperity: Successful management of economic devastation lays the groundwork for long-term prosperity. By addressing challenges head-on, societies can overcome obstacles, develop new avenues for growth, and create an environment conducive to inclusive and sustainable economic development.

Addressing economic devastation is not merely a matter of fiscal policy but a moral, social, and strategic imperative. It impacts the well-being of citizens, the stability of societies, and the potential for future growth. By taking comprehensive and well-targeted actions, nations can not only mitigate the immediate impact of economic distress but also pave the way for a more resilient, inclusive, and prosperous future.

Economic Shocks and Crises: Economic shocks and crises are potent triggers of economic devastation, capable of disrupting the delicate balance of economic systems and leading to widespread turmoil. These shocks can emerge from various sources, ranging from financial vulnerabilities to global events, and their effects often cascade through economies, leaving lasting scars. Here's an in-depth exploration of how economic shocks and crises can cause and indicate economic devastation:

Causes:

1. Financial Crises: Sudden disruptions in the financial sector, such as banking failures, stock

market crashes, or a credit crunch, can trigger a chain reaction that undermines economic stability. When trust in financial institutions erodes, it can lead to reduced investment, capital flight, and credit freezes, causing a severe contraction in economic activity.

2. Asset Bubbles Bursting: Rapidly inflating asset prices, such as real estate or stock markets, followed by their sudden collapse, can lead to economic devastation. The bursting of asset bubbles can result in significant wealth loss, reduced consumer spending, and financial instability.

3. Debt Crises: Excessive public or private debt can become unsustainable, leading to defaults, credit rating downgrades, and a loss of investor confidence. Debt crises can constrain governments'

ability to provide essential services and stimulate economic growth.

Indicators:

1. GDP Contraction: One of the most direct indicators of economic devastation is a sharp decline in Gross Domestic Product (GDP). Economic shocks and crises often lead to decreased production, lower consumer spending, and reduced investment, resulting in negative GDP growth.
2. Rising Unemployment: Economic shocks can swiftly translate into job losses as businesses cut costs and reduce operations. Elevated unemployment rates not only contribute to human suffering but also weaken purchasing power, leading to a downward spiral in economic activity.

3. Stock Market Volatility: Extreme fluctuations in stock markets can signal investor uncertainty and rapidly erode wealth. Significant drops in stock prices can lead to reduced business investment, pension fund losses, and reduced consumer confidence.
4. Bank Runs and Credit Crunches: In financial crises, individuals rushing to withdraw their funds from banks can trigger bank runs. This strains banking institutions, leading to a credit crunch where businesses and consumers struggle to access loans and credit.
5. Currency Devaluation: Economic crises can lead to a rapid depreciation of a country's currency. This can raise import costs, exacerbate inflation, and impact external trade relations.

6. Sovereign Debt Downgrades: Credit rating agencies may downgrade a nation's sovereign debt rating due to concerns about its ability to meet debt obligations. This can increase borrowing costs and reduce investor confidence.

Addressing the causes and mitigating the indicators of economic shocks and crises require a combination of prudent fiscal and monetary policies, effective regulatory measures, and international cooperation. Successfully navigating these challenges hinges on timely and well-coordinated responses that restore confidence, stabilize financial systems, and pave the way for sustainable economic recovery.

Economic devastation extends its reach far beyond financial statistics and economic indicators, profoundly affecting both societies as a whole and the lives of individuals within those societies. The ripples of economic turmoil touch upon various dimensions of human existence, from financial well-being to mental health, and even to the social fabric that binds communities together. Here's an in-depth exploration of how economic devastation impacts society and individuals:

Impact on Society:

1. Increased Poverty and Inequality: Economic devastation often exacerbates existing social disparities and leads to an increase

in poverty rates. As jobs are lost and incomes decline, more individuals and families struggle to meet basic needs, leading to a widening wealth gap within society.

2. Social Unrest and Political Instability: A population grappling with economic hardship may become more susceptible to social unrest, protests, and demonstrations. When individuals perceive economic injustices, political instability can follow, potentially leading to a breakdown of governance structures.

3. Pressure on Social Services: As more people face financial difficulties, there is an increased demand for social safety nets, healthcare, and other essential services. The strain on government resources can lead to challenges in

maintaining quality services and adequate support systems.

4. Impact on Education: Economic devastation can hinder access to quality education, as families struggle to afford schooling and universities face funding cuts. The long-term consequences include reduced human capital development and decreased opportunities for upward mobility.

5. Healthcare Challenges: A deteriorating economy can limit access to healthcare, resulting in reduced healthcare infrastructure, medication shortages, and increased stress on healthcare professionals.

6. Migration and Brain Drain: Economic devastation can prompt individuals to seek better opportunities elsewhere, leading to emigration and potentially causing

a "brain drain" as skilled workers leave the country.

Impact on Individuals:

1. Loss of Livelihoods: One of the most direct impacts of economic devastation on individuals is the loss of jobs and income. Unemployment and underemployment can lead to financial stress, affecting the ability to cover basic needs.

2. Mental Health Challenges: Economic hardship can trigger mental health issues such as anxiety, depression, and increased stress levels. Uncertainty about the future, financial strain, and the loss of a stable routine can take a toll on individuals' well-being.

3. Diminished Quality of Life: Reduced income and limited access to resources can lead to a

decline in individuals' quality of life, impacting everything from housing to nutrition and leisure activities.

4. Family Dynamics: Financial stress can strain family relationships and increase conflicts. Parents may struggle to provide for their children, affecting their well-being and prospects.

5. Delayed Life Goals: Economic devastation can postpone or shatter individuals' life goals, whether it's buying a home, pursuing higher education, starting a family, or saving for retirement.

6. Lack of Economic Mobility: Individuals facing economic devastation might find it difficult to transition to better economic circumstances due to limited opportunities and resources.

Addressing the societal and individual impacts of economic devastation requires comprehensive measures that go beyond economic policies. A holistic approach involves fostering social support networks, prioritizing mental health services, ensuring access to education and healthcare, and implementing targeted programs to alleviate poverty and inequality. By recognizing the human aspect of economic distress and designing interventions accordingly, societies can better navigate the challenges brought about by economic turmoil and lay the foundation for recovery and resilience.

Government Interventions: When economic devastation strikes, governments play a pivotal role in stabilizing and revitalizing the economy. Government interventions are critical for mitigating the immediate impact of economic shocks, protecting vulnerable populations, and fostering an environment conducive to recovery and sustainable growth. These interventions encompass a range of fiscal and monetary measures that collectively aim to restore confidence, stimulate economic activity, and lay the groundwork for long-term resilience. Here's an in-depth exploration of government interventions as strategies for recovery and rebuilding:

1. Fiscal Stimulus Packages:

Governments inject funds into the economy through increased government spending on infrastructure projects, public services, and welfare programs.

Tax cuts or rebates provide individuals and businesses with more disposable income, boosting consumer spending and business investment.

Direct cash transfers to households help alleviate financial distress, stimulate demand, and support those most affected by economic devastation.

2. Monetary Policy Adjustments:

Central banks lower interest rates to encourage borrowing, business investment, and consumer spending.

Quantitative easing involves purchasing financial assets to increase the money supply and improve liquidity in financial markets.

Forward guidance communicates the central bank's intentions to maintain an accommodative monetary policy to boost confidence and investment.

3. Social Safety Nets:

The expansion of unemployment benefits helps individuals who have lost jobs due to economic shocks, providing financial assistance during their job search.

Food assistance programs ensure access to nutrition for vulnerable populations, reducing the impact of poverty and hunger.

4. Debt Relief and Restructuring:

Governments can negotiate debt relief or restructuring agreements with creditors, providing breathing room for struggling economies.

Debt moratoriums allow countries to temporarily halt debt payments, redirecting resources towards critical services and recovery efforts.

5. Infrastructure Investment:

Government-led infrastructure projects create jobs, stimulate demand for materials and services, and contribute to long-term economic growth.

Investments in sustainable and green infrastructure align recovery efforts with environmental goals.

6. Business Support and Incentives:

Small and medium-sized enterprises (SMEs) receive financial assistance, grants, or loans to help them weather economic challenges and retain employees.

Incentives for research and development encourage innovation and new business ventures, fostering long-term competitiveness.

7. Labor Market Policies:

Job training and reskilling programs help unemployed individuals acquire new skills to reenter the workforce.

Work-sharing programs allow companies to reduce working hours while the government subsidizes part of employees' lost wages.

8. Consumer and Investor Confidence Building:

Transparency in government actions and communication about recovery plans boost confidence in economic prospects.

Regulatory reforms and measures to enhance governance and accountability improve investor sentiment.

Government interventions need to be well-targeted, adaptive, and aligned with the unique challenges posed by specific economic shocks. Effective execution requires coordination among different government agencies, clear communication with the public, and monitoring of the interventions' impact on various sectors. By employing a mix of fiscal and monetary tools, governments can play a crucial role in jumpstarting economic activity, rebuilding shattered industries, and steering economies toward a path of sustained recovery and growth.

Structural Reforms

In the wake of economic devastation, structural reforms emerge as potent strategies for rejuvenating economies, fostering long-term resilience, and addressing underlying vulnerabilities that contributed to the crisis. These reforms encompass targeted changes to economic, regulatory, and institutional frameworks, aiming to promote efficiency, competitiveness, and sustainable growth. By addressing systemic weaknesses and encouraging innovation, structural reforms lay the groundwork for a more robust and adaptive economy. Here's an in-depth exploration of structural reforms as strategies for recovery and rebuilding:

1. Diversification of Industries:

Encouraging the development of multiple industries reduces overreliance on a single sector, mitigating the impact of future shocks.

Investment in emerging sectors, such as technology, renewable energy, and healthcare, positions the economy for future growth and job creation.

2. Business Environment Improvement:

Streamlining bureaucratic procedures, reducing red tape, and simplifying regulations make it easier for businesses to operate and innovate.

Efficient and transparent regulatory frameworks attract investment and foster entrepreneurship.

3. Labor Market Flexibility:

Labor market reforms that balance the rights of employees and employers enable businesses to adapt to changing circumstances more effectively.

Flexible labor laws can encourage job creation, workforce reskilling, and more efficient resource allocation.

4. Innovation and Research Support:

Investment in research and development fosters innovation, which is vital for adapting to new market dynamics and technological shifts.

Encouraging collaboration between academia, research institutions, and the private sector accelerates innovation.

5. Public Sector Reforms:

Improving the efficiency and effectiveness of public services enhances the government's capacity to respond to crises and deliver essential services.

Anti-corruption measures and good governance practices restore public trust and promote accountability.

6. Trade and Investment Liberalization:

Opening up markets to international trade and investment creates opportunities for businesses to expand, access new markets, and diversify revenue sources.

Bilateral and multilateral trade agreements facilitate cross-border commerce and improve economic integration.

7. Infrastructure Development:

Investing in critical infrastructure, such as transportation, energy, and digital networks, supports economic activities and enhances connectivity.

Modern infrastructure attracts investment, boosts productivity, and stimulates economic growth.

8. Financial Sector Reforms:

Strengthening regulatory oversight and enhancing financial stability safeguards against future crises and maintains investor confidence.

Promoting inclusive financial services extends access to banking and credit, benefiting individuals and businesses.

9. Education and Human Capital Enhancement:

Improving the quality and relevance of education equips the workforce with the skills needed for evolving industries.

Lifelong learning initiatives help individuals adapt to changing job market demands.

Implementing structural reforms requires careful planning, stakeholder engagement, and a comprehensive understanding of the country's unique challenges. Policymakers must strike a balance between short-term recovery measures and long-term structural adjustments. Successful reforms are often accompanied by effective communication, monitoring, and adaptation to ensure their positive impact. By embracing structural reforms, nations can not only recover from economic devastation but also create a more dynamic, competitive, and resilient economy poised for sustainable growth.

In the face of economic devastation, nations often turn to international cooperation and aid as strategies for accelerating recovery and rebuilding. Collaborative efforts between countries, international organizations, and development partners can provide vital resources, expertise, and support that complement domestic efforts. These strategies foster solidarity, enhance global stability, and contribute to the shared goal of restoring economic health and prosperity. Here's an in-depth exploration of international cooperation and aid as strategies for recovery and rebuilding:

1. Multilateral Organizations' Role:

Organizations like the International Monetary Fund (IMF), World Bank, and United Nations provide financial assistance, technical expertise, and policy guidance to countries in crisis.

Programs from these organizations can offer essential liquidity, facilitate structural reforms, and stabilize financial markets.

2. Bilateral Assistance and Partnerships:

Governments and international partners extend bilateral assistance, offering grants, concessional loans, or technical support tailored to a country's specific needs.

Collaborative partnerships between developed and developing nations leverage resources, knowledge, and experience for mutual benefit.

3. Debt Relief and Rescheduling:

International efforts to provide debt relief or reschedule debt payments alleviate the burden on countries facing economic distress.

Debt relief allows nations to redirect resources toward recovery and social development.

4. Trade and Investment Promotion:

Bilateral and regional trade agreements can stimulate economic activity by expanding market access, boosting exports, and attracting foreign investment.

Investment promotion agencies facilitate partnerships between foreign investors and domestic industries.

5. Technology and Knowledge Transfer:

Collaborative research and technology transfer agreements enable countries to access innovations, expertise, and best practices from partners with advanced capabilities.

6. Humanitarian Assistance and Aid:

Humanitarian aid provides immediate relief by addressing critical needs, such as food, shelter, and healthcare, in the aftermath of crises.

Aid organizations and countries collaborate to ensure timely and effective distribution of assistance.

7. Capacity Building and Training:

International training programs and capacity-building initiatives help strengthen institutions, improve governance, and enhance human resources for effective recovery.

8. Crisis Preparedness and Early Warning Systems:

International collaboration on monitoring economic indicators and sharing information helps countries prepare for potential crises and take preventive measures.

9. Global Financial Stability Measures:

Central banks and international organizations coordinate to stabilize global financial markets, ensuring that economic turmoil in one country does not trigger broader instability.

Successful international cooperation and aid require open communication, shared objectives, and mutual respect among nations. Partnerships should be based on a genuine commitment to equitable distribution of benefits, respect for sovereignty, and alignment with a country's development priorities. Effective implementation involves clear agreements, monitoring mechanisms, and the flexibility to adapt strategies as circumstances evolve. By coming together in times of economic distress, countries can pool their resources, knowledge, and strengths to achieve more impactful and sustainable recovery outcomes for the benefit of all.

Throughout history, several nations have faced and successfully overcome economic devastation, demonstrating resilience, innovative strategies, and effective policies. These case studies offer valuable insights into how countries can navigate the challenges of economic turmoil and emerge stronger on the other side. Here are three notable examples:

Germany after World War II:

Situation: Post-World War II, Germany was left devastated, with cities in ruins, infrastructure destroyed, and an economy in shambles.

Strategies for Recovery:

- The Marshall Plan: Germany benefited from the European

Recovery Program, commonly known as the Marshall Plan, which provided financial aid to rebuild infrastructure, stimulate trade, and modernize industries.

- Currency Reform: Germany introduced the Deutsche Mark (DM) as a stable currency, curbing hyperinflation and restoring confidence in the financial system.
- Industrial Decentralization: To diversify the economy and reduce vulnerability, industries were decentralized across the country, fostering regional development.
- Impact and Outcome: Within a decade, Germany emerged as an economic powerhouse, fueled by industrial growth, technological advancement, and a highly skilled workforce. The "Wirtschaftswunder" (economic miracle) propelled Germany's

transformation into a leading global economy.

Iceland's Recovery from the Financial Crisis (2008-2011):

Situation: Iceland faced a severe financial crisis in 2008, characterized by a banking collapse, a plummeting currency, and soaring unemployment.

Strategies for Recovery:

- Financial Restructuring: The government placed major banks into receivership, ring-fencing domestic assets, and assuming control of key sectors.
- Austerity and Social Support: While implementing austerity measures, Iceland also focused on protecting vulnerable citizens through social support programs.
- Currency Stabilization: The central bank worked to stabilize the

Icelandic Krona (ISK) and control inflation.

- Impact and Outcome: Iceland's focus on social cohesion, economic restructuring, and financial stabilization helped it rebound relatively quickly. The country implemented strict capital controls, prioritized financial sector reforms, and eventually restored investor confidence.

Rwanda's Post-Genocide Economic Transformation:

Situation: After the 1994 genocide, Rwanda faced widespread devastation, loss of life, and societal trauma.

Strategies for Recovery:

- Vision 2020: Rwanda adopted a long-term development plan emphasizing economic diversification, poverty reduction, and sustainable growth.

- Investment in Human Capital: Education and healthcare were prioritized to develop a skilled workforce and improve overall well-being.
- Infrastructure Development: Rwanda invested in transportation, energy, and telecommunications infrastructure to facilitate business activities.
- Impact and Outcome: Through visionary leadership and strategic planning, Rwanda achieved remarkable progress. The country's focus on promoting tourism, agriculture, and services has led to sustained economic growth and poverty reduction. Social reconciliation efforts and investments in women's

empowerment have contributed to social stability and progress.

These case studies highlight the transformative power of resilience, innovative policies, and strong leadership. They underscore the importance of embracing a multifaceted approach that includes fiscal, monetary, and structural reforms, as well as international cooperation. By learning from these examples, countries can glean valuable lessons on how to navigate adversity, rebuild shattered economies, and lay the foundation for a more prosperous and stable future.

The stories of countries that have successfully overcome economic devastation offer valuable lessons and best practices for navigating crises, fostering recovery, and building resilient economies. Drawing from these experiences can guide policymakers, leaders, and societies in responding effectively to challenges and charting a path toward sustainable growth. Here are key lessons learned and best practices:

1. Strong Leadership and Vision:

- Visionary leadership that prioritizes long-term goals and national interests is crucial during times of crisis.

- Leaders should communicate, instill confidence, and guide the nation through difficult decisions.

2. Swift and Coordinated Action:

- Prompt and coordinated responses are essential to stabilize the economy, restore confidence, and prevent further damage.
- Governments must collaborate with international partners, central banks, and key stakeholders.

3. Inclusive Approaches:

- Policies must be designed with inclusivity in mind, protecting vulnerable populations and ensuring equitable benefits.
- Inclusive growth promotes social cohesion and reduces inequalities, enhancing long-term stability.

4. Diversification and Adaptability:

- Diversifying industries and revenue sources reduces dependency on a single sector, enhancing economic resilience.

- Adaptability to changing market dynamics allows countries to seize emerging opportunities and manage risks.

5. Investment in Human Capital:

- Prioritizing education, healthcare, and skill development equips the workforce for evolving industries.
- A skilled and healthy workforce is a foundation for sustainable growth.

6. Innovation and Technology:

- Embracing innovation and technological advancements fosters economic transformation and competitiveness.
- Encouraging research, development, and entrepreneurship drives resilience and new economic opportunities.

7. Transparency and Accountability:

- Transparent governance builds trust and credibility, ensuring that policies are well-informed and accountable.
- Anti-corruption measures are critical to maintain public trust and allocate resources efficiently.

8. Balancing Short-Term Relief and Long-Term Recovery:

- Governments should balance short-term relief measures with structural reforms for sustained recovery.
- Resilient economies are built through a combination of immediate responses and forward-looking strategies.

9. International Cooperation and Aid:

- Collaborating with international partners and institutions can provide essential resources, expertise, and support.

- Bilateral and multilateral efforts enhance recovery prospects and reinforce global stability.

10.   Community Engagement and Social Reconciliation:

- Building strong social bonds through community engagement, dialogue, and reconciliation contributes to stability.
- Addressing historical grievances and fostering unity promotes social cohesion and progress.

11.   Sustainability and Environmental Considerations:

- Integrate sustainability into recovery efforts by promoting green technologies, renewable energy, and responsible resource management.
- Sustainable practices ensure long-term economic viability and minimize negative impacts on the environment.

12. Adaptive Resilience:
- Building adaptive capacity allows countries to withstand shocks, learn from challenges, and innovate for the future.
- Continuous monitoring, evaluation, and adjustment of strategies are essential components of resilience.

In navigating economic devastation, there is no one-size-fits-all approach. The lessons learned from various case studies underscore the importance of tailored strategies that address a nation's unique context and challenges. By embracing a combination of sound policies, inclusive approaches, and innovative thinking, countries can emerge from crises with renewed strength, laying the foundation for a more prosperous and resilient future.

As the world faces increasing uncertainties, future-proofing against economic devastation is a vital imperative for nations seeking stability and prosperity. To safeguard economies from the impact of crises and unexpected shocks, countries must adopt proactive strategies that enhance resilience, promote adaptability, and ensure sustainable growth. Here's a comprehensive guide to future-proofing against economic devastation:

1. Diversified Economy:
- Cultivate a diverse economic base with multiple thriving industries to reduce dependency on a single sector.

- Invest in emerging industries and technologies to stay ahead of market shifts.

2. Agile Policy Frameworks:

- Develop flexible policy frameworks that can quickly adapt to changing circumstances.
- Implement scenario-based planning to anticipate and prepare for various economic challenges.

3. Investment in Education and Innovation:

- Foster a culture of innovation by investing in research, development, and education.
- Nurture a skilled workforce that can drive technological advancements and contribute to economic transformation.

4. Infrastructure Development:

- Invest in modern and resilient infrastructure to support economic activities and connectivity.

- Prioritize sustainability and adaptability in infrastructure planning.

5. Social Safety Nets:

- Strengthen social safety nets to provide a buffer for vulnerable populations during economic downturns.
- Ensure that essential services, such as healthcare and education, remain accessible.

6. Diversified Trade Relationships:

- Expand and diversify trade relationships to reduce reliance on a single market.
- Pursue bilateral and multilateral agreements that enhance economic integration.

7. Sustainable Practices:

- Embed sustainability into economic strategies to mitigate environmental risks and ensure long-term viability.

- Promote renewable energy, responsible resource management, and circular economy initiatives.

8. Digital Transformation:

- Embrace digitalization to enhance efficiency, competitiveness, and access to global markets.
- Foster a digital-ready workforce through upskilling and digital education programs.

9. Economic Inclusion and Equality:

- Address income inequality and social disparities to promote social cohesion and stability.
- Ensure that economic growth benefits all segments of society.

10. Financial Resilience:

- Maintain sound fiscal policies and build sufficient fiscal buffers during periods of economic growth.
- Strengthen financial institutions and regulatory frameworks to withstand shocks.

11.   Crisis Preparedness:

- Develop robust crisis management and early warning systems to detect and respond to emerging risks.
- Regularly simulate crisis scenarios to test the effectiveness of response strategies.

12.   Strengthening Governance:

- Promote transparent and accountable governance practices to build public trust and ensure efficient resource allocation.
- Implement anti-corruption measures to prevent misuse of public funds.

13.   Partnerships and Cooperation:

- Collaborate with international partners, organizations, and neighboring countries to share knowledge, resources, and best practices.

- Seek support and aid during times of crisis through bilateral and multilateral channels.

Future-proofing against economic devastation requires a holistic and proactive approach. It entails continuous learning, adaptability, and a willingness to challenge traditional norms. By embracing a comprehensive strategy that integrates economic, social, environmental, and technological considerations, nations can bolster their resilience, minimize vulnerabilities, and create a more sustainable and prosperous future for their citizens.

In times of economic devastation, when traditional pathways to success are disrupted, individuals face unique challenges. However, adversity can also spark innovation and drive personal growth. These are practical strategies that individuals can adopt to not only survive but thrive during economic downturns.

Embracing a Growth Mindset: A Strategy for Individual Success Amidst Economic Devastation

In times of economic devastation, cultivating a growth mindset becomes a powerful strategy for individuals to navigate challenges, adapt to changes, and position themselves for success. A growth mindset is a belief that abilities and skills can be developed through dedication, effort, and continuous learning. By adopting this mindset, individuals can not only overcome obstacles but also thrive amidst adversity. Here's an in-depth exploration of how embracing a growth mindset contributes to individual success during economic devastation:

1. Adapting to Change:
- Individuals with a growth mindset are more adaptable to changes in the economic landscape.
- They see challenges as opportunities to learn and improve, making them better equipped to navigate uncertainties.

2. Resilience and Persistence:
- A growth mindset encourages individuals to persist in the face of setbacks.
- They view failures as stepping stones to success and use

setbacks as valuable learning experiences.

3. Continuous Learning:

- Those with a growth mindset embrace learning as a lifelong journey.
- They seek new skills, knowledge, and experiences, positioning themselves to seize emerging opportunities.

4. Innovation and Creativity:

- A growth mindset fosters innovative thinking and creative problem-solving.
- Individuals are more likely to explore new solutions and approaches to challenges.

5. Building Self-Efficacy:

- Individuals with a growth mindset develop a sense of self-efficacy, believing in their ability to influence their outcomes.

- This confidence empowers them to take initiative and pursue new avenues.

6. Embracing Challenges:

- Instead of avoiding challenges, individuals with a growth mindset embrace them as opportunities for growth.
- They are more likely to step out of their comfort zones and tackle difficult tasks.

7. Collaboration and Networking:

- Those with a growth mindset value collaboration and seek opportunities to learn from others.
- They build strong networks, which can offer support, insights, and potential partnerships.

8. Goal Orientation:

- A growth mindset encourages individuals to set ambitious goals and work persistently toward achieving them.

- They view goals as achievable through effort and dedication.

9. Managing Stress and Anxiety:

- Embracing a growth mindset reduces fear of failure and helps individuals manage stress and anxiety.

- They focus on growth and improvement, rather than being overwhelmed by negative emotions.

10. Staying Positive and Motivated:

* A growth mindset promotes a positive outlook and intrinsic motivation.

* Individuals remain engaged, enthusiastic, and driven to achieve their aspirations.

In the face of economic devastation, embracing a growth mindset empowers individuals to take control of their trajectories. This mindset shift is a catalyst for personal development and success, enabling individuals to thrive despite challenging circumstances. By focusing on self-improvement, adaptability, and continuous learning, individuals can turn adversity into opportunities and emerge stronger, more resilient, and better equipped to excel in any economic landscape.

I. Mindset:

A. Develop a positive and adaptable attitude towards change.

B. View challenges as opportunities for learning and self-improvement.

C. Seek out new skills and knowledge to stay relevant in evolving industries.

II. Diversify Skills and Knowledge:

A. Identify transferable skills that can be applied across various industries.

B. Pursue online courses, workshops, and certifications to expand your skill set.

C. Become a lifelong learner to remain agile in a rapidly changing job market.

III. Build a Resilient Financial Plan:

A. Create a budget and prioritize essential expenses.

B. Build an emergency fund to cushion against unexpected financial shocks.

C. Explore additional income streams, such as freelancing, consulting, or part-time work.

IV. Cultivate a Professional Network:

A. Maintain and nurture relationships with colleagues, mentors, and industry peers.

B. Attend networking events, conferences, and webinars to stay connected.

C. Networking can open doors to new opportunities and collaborations.

V. Harness Entrepreneurial Spirit:

A. Identify gaps in the market and explore entrepreneurial ventures.

B. Start a small business, leveraging your skills and passions.

C. Entrepreneurship offers flexibility and the potential for creating multiple income streams.

VI. Focus on Personal Branding:

A. Build a strong online presence through social media and personal websites.

B. Showcase your skills, accomplishments, and expertise to stand out to potential employers or clients.

C. Personal branding can enhance visibility and attract opportunities.

VII. Adaptability and Agility:

A. Embrace change and quickly pivot in response to shifting market dynamics.

B. Be open to exploring different roles or industries that align with your skills.

C. Agility enables individuals to navigate uncertainty and capitalize on emerging trends.

VIII. Prioritize Mental and Physical Well-being:

A. Practice self-care routines to manage stress and maintain mental clarity.

B. Engage in regular exercise and maintain a healthy lifestyle.

C. Well-being is essential for maintaining focus, creativity, and resilience.

IX. Volunteer and Give Back:

A. Contribute to your community through volunteering or mentorship.

B. Giving back can provide a sense of purpose and f74ulfilmentduring challenging times.

C. Volunteering can also help expand your network and showcase your skills.

Economic devastation can be a challenging and uncertain time for individuals, but taking proactive precautions can help mitigate its impact and position you for recovery and success. Whether you"e navigating the crisis itself or working towards rebuilding afterward, here are some best precautions to consider:

During Economic Devastation:

1. Assess Financial Situation:
- Evaluate your current financial state, including savings, expenses, and debts.
- Prioritize essential expenses and consider cutting discretionary spending.
2. Diversify Income Sources:

- If possible, explore additional income streams or part-time work to supplement your earnings.
- Consider freelancing, remote work, or starting a small business to increase financial stability.

3. Build Emergency Fund:

- Set aside funds in an emergency savings account to cover essential expenses in case of job loss or unexpected expenses.
- Aim for at least three to six months' worth of living expenses.

4. Networking and Skill Enhancement:

- Strengthen your professional network by staying connected with colleagues, mentors, and industry contacts.
- Use downtime to enhance your skills through online courses, workshops, or certifications.

5. Stay Informed:

- Keep abreast of economic developments and policy changes that may affect your industry or financial situation.
- Being well-informed can help you make informed decisions.

After Economic Devastation:

1. Reevaluate Financial Goals:
- Take stock of your financial goals and adjust them based on the current economic landscape.
- Prioritize short-term stability while keeping long-term objectives in mind.

2. Debt Management:
- Prioritize paying off high-interest debts to reduce financial burden.
- Explore consolidation or negotiation options to make debt management more manageable.

3. Invest in Education and Skill Development:

- Invest in acquiring new skills that align with evolving market demands.
- Continuous learning enhances your employability and adaptability.

4. Diversify Investments:
- If you're investing, diversify your portfolio to spread risk across different asset classes.
- Consult a financial advisor for personalized investment advice.

5. Retirement Planning:
- Continue contributing to retirement accounts, such as 401(k)s or IRAs, to ensure long-term financial security.
- Adjust your contributions based on your current financial situation.

6. Maintain Emergency Fund:
- Even after the crisis subsides, keep your emergency fund intact to prepare for any future uncertainties.

- This fund provides a safety net during unexpected events.

7. Professional Networking:

- Maintain and nurture your professional network to stay connected with opportunities and industry trends.
- Networking can open doors for career advancement and collaboration.

8. Adopt Frugality and Budgeting:

- Continue practicing mindful spending and budgeting to maintain financial discipline.
- Frugality can help you build a strong financial foundation.

9. Health and Well-being:

- Prioritize physical and mental health to maintain resilience during challenges.
- A healthy lifestyle contributes to your overall well-being and productivity.

10. Stay Positive and Resilient:

- Maintain a positive outlook and embrace challenges as opportunities for growth.
- Cultivate resilience to adapt to changing circumstances and bounce back from setbacks.

By taking these precautions, you empower yourself to navigate economic devastation with greater confidence and resilience. While the road may be challenging, being proactive about your financial well-being and personal development can make a significant difference in your ability to recover, rebuild, and thrive in the long run.

Conclusion

Economic devastation might present hurdles, but it also offers opportunities for personal and professional growth. By adopting a proactive and adaptable mindset, diversifying skills, building a resilient financial plan, and staying connected within your network, you can not only weather the storm but also come out stronger on the other side. Remember that individual success during tough economic times often stems from innovation, perseverance, and a commitment to continuous improvement.